The Lifelong Ramblings Of The Imperfect Greying Man

CW01584108

Contents

Foreword (to forearm)

We all try, in our own ways, to make sense of our world.

Over the years, from boy to teen to man, I've tried to convey some of my thoughts and feelings onto paper, as I seek and explore, mainly through the medium of poetry.

I hope you like it.

Inspired to do this by Rhian (and Nancy), by Claire and Geraint (and Liz), who have shared some of this with me, sometimes for better, sometimes for worse; who have likely seen the best, and the worst of this imperfect man.

With special thanks to Mari Lewis, Aled Jones and Dewi Morgan Evans, whose passion and encouragement did actually make a difference to a troubled young man; and to Mrs Gwen Parry Jones, who believed in me when I was 7 years old.

And to some who have occasionally, touched and impacted on my life for the better, you'll hopefully know who you are: Heddwen, Bethan, BJ, Jimmy, Carole, Howard, Alison, Eric, Toni, Brian, Gerallt, Erwin, Rags, Jason, Steve, Willie.

From our first, our Fathers, to last Amen,

We despise the imperfect greying men.

They sow testament, in their serious tones,

Seeding sediment from their lofty thrones;

Impregnating minds, terminal trammel,

Fabricated heav'n, an eternal Hell...

Wide eyed look around, then increasing phlegm...

Realised, 'Oh Shit!'... I'm now one of them.

The Calendar

Is poison's stem... pursuit of time
The measurement by which we climb?
Compare, contrast, curtail and cost
For happiness we sought and lost?

Finite, by night, we tear off days
At pace forbidding time appraised
As past is thrown, as pastures sought
Is happiness found in aforethought?

For as men wait for time and space
Their dreams discharged, at calendar pace
Those lost small moments, consigned to past
Sought happiness seen fading fast

Seek happiness... all rushing fools
When cycling blind by calendar rules
They may not find green future pleasant...
For happiness hides 'tween past and present

Easter Sunday (in the virus)

Easter Sunday.
I am risen, early
To paint the front door
Black.
As the moor
Of my mood

Repainting drips
Is an unsatisfactory
Activity
So, legs a'crossed,
Smelling of gloss
I sit and watch
A view
Of captivity

Umpteen joggers escape..
They bounce like babies,
The puffing ladies
And pink gin faced men.

The surely illicit..
Young couple
Feeling invisible,
Invincible forever
As they hug and kiss goodbyes
Two metres together

Blue flashing...
The occasional ambulance,
Silently passing
An occasional curse.
I while and wonder...
What's worse?
Sooner...
Or later?

Embedded in my humanity
I watch my world go by
Bye bye

You Really Got Me

Near homely single bed, near teenage dreams

Sat night-blue booming, bass… on my player

A path too Rotten, from Leo Sayer

Evokes cold Christmas, spills bright summer beams

Bouncing with Blondie, that temptress of teens

Bowie pours downward - influence layers;

Aretha charms, we say a little prayer

For short sharp shot sexting three-minute themes:

Charging, rough, ready; it's muggy and moist

Familiar for feisty, the British love bite

By your side; with purpose, spat out and voiced

Unsentimental, a man in the light

Kinky and kicking, bright fistful of noise

Throws out a boy’s passion, he can’t sleep at night…

Lost Love

In our guarded hearts:

Undermining,

Reinforcing,

Unforgiving

Our human frailties

Our lost Love sits everywhere

In my stifled mourning tears,

I am strangely comforted

By images of baked camembert

Of stirring morning coffee,

By the memorable colours

Of prison castle courtyard greys,

By Orme greens,

Never forgotten laburnum yellows

I fold all these tenderly,

As I once...

Held your hand...

Stroked your face...

Touched your lips...

At the kissing gates

(continued...)

To store in my heart,

Fondly,

Alongside a picture of you –

My lost love

Orange Light

During that winter

Of discontent..

Drab and discordant

The Orange Peel's

Orange light

Shed desolate...

Life was,

As it seemed,

A little bit shite

The Orange Peel Disco

Cast a tired beacon

Of ghastly, ghostly tunes.

It glittered orange light

On the littered, empty seafront

Of our lives.

Ironically, maybe..

Gloria sang..

I will survive

(continued...)

Blocky, knuckled bouncers
Bearing black bleak suits
In wooden keep
Seemingly immune
To slicing cold winds
That sleet and sweep
Across a car starved West Parade
From a grey opposing sea

They wait to see
Which hopefully hopeless
Eye lined young men,
With tee shirt and ring in ear,
Drawn by
Foolish young girls in socks
Who may never appear,
And orange light;
By vague Promises,
And the Buzzcocks...

(continued...)

As a still foolish

Old young man...

When I dream

Of orange light

And Orange Peel...

The cold is gone,

The waves are still

And stranger still,

Recalling..

Salty sounds and smells

And desperate times,

I miss...

That bleak Octobered Rhyl

I smile,

Despite the time...

Because that future then...

That orange light..

Was mine

The Dissection

I am the dissection;

And my life...

A concept.

Defined finite

By your own...

Context.

Manfully,

Painfully,

Playfully...

You pull me apart...

Butterfly wing

By butterfly wing

I am splayed,

I am spayed,

I am sexed,

I am exposed.

As I doze...

You dissect..

(continued...)

Medusan you rise...

(Not of your sex,

But androgynous guise)

You stone and dissect...

I decay...

Full frontal,

In your eyes

I became space,

A genocide race,

A series

Of the interlaced.

Still-judged;

Both revived and reviled

Those snapshots of my

Still-life, you see.

Those bedraggled pieces,

That are me;

Like my poet,

Sit unravelled,

Sit disheveled

They, and I,

No longer fit...

Into a hole.

My whole ceases,

For the others..

To you..

I am simply...

Pieces

ʹlack Angry (A view from outside)

ʹhis poem was written in 2020 after the death of George Floyd in Minneapolis, USA. The ʹrevailing mood led my mind back to almost twenty years earlier, when my then girlfriend, a ʹrong and beautiful black woman, was racially abused by a group of young men in a taxi. ʹhe was pushing our daughter in a pushchair at the time.

ı the pushchair

watched my mother cry

t monkey noises

rom cars passing by

ı the playgroup

ıformed that I was black

young informer

ouldn't take it back

ı the playground

/e fought the youthful fight

hey called me "nigger"

I beat them right

n the pavement

/ide-passed; passed suspicion

een skin blazed bad;

ı innocent perdition

ontinued...)

In the workplace

Beyond my African name

They mispronounce me

I feel their pain..

Black angry?

Not all of the time...

Sensitive?

Doesn't even fucking rhyme...

Dancing for the family

It's complicated:

Manically,

We dance like fools

But seriously?..

That routine series

Of quicksteps

Navigating our

Righteous, roiled pools

Of unspoken detritus.

Unchallenged, we glide on

Past heartfelt barriers,

Skilfully weaving, leaving aside...

Because it's comfortable,

We coexist...

In perpetual and familiar infamy

Because it's them...

And it's us...

The family.

Night

At dark nights approaching

Could you hold my hand

As strong grasp, sands slipping,

From familiar land?

Will your love be blessing

Will it ease my fear,

Be balm, sound and lighting

In dead, dark, atmosphere?

When my eyes are closing

As my ears...

Slow deaf...

Can my knowledge of you

Ease my final breath?

As the days get shorter

To the night unknown

May I hold you tightly

Your softness...

My touchstone?

(continued...)

Tender touch, a'suppling,

Practised little deaths

Glad, upon uncoupling

That I didn't...

Swipe left.

The Greatest

An old man moves with quiet sighs,

Uncertain mischief in his eyes;

Slow and stilted, shakes a fist

Defiant yet at life's cruel kiss

Head once held proud, to spite blank slurs

Now lowered, muted, by the years

Yet hero holds, and eyes hold fast:

A man of stature, fit to last

At twelve, his youthful, deathly choice

Produced a brief, eternal voice

By race defined, by hardship honed;

Showed sharp, stilettoed, smart, intoned

Once swift of lip, yet swifter still

Of thought, and pugilistic skill

In equal parts, an equal duel

Of charismatic, cool... and cruel

There lies my greatest, his final bout

With past unbroken, despite fate's drought

My schoolboy wonder, open ears...

The old man lying disappears

Replaced by one, when standing tall

Rogues, racists, jailers... beat them all

As inspiration, sold my hope

That one day I might 'rope-a-dope'

When stripped of titles, dying slow

Is man expunged by life's low blow?

Or like The Greatest, when I die

Will my hope float, like a butterfly?

The Clock

Consider a mantlepiece

Imagine then...

In your twilight

Those dead stares..

From black and white

Alongside,

Beside... that ticking clock.

Consider the second hand

Tocking away...

A moment's death

An expired sound

Of ultimate breath

Stifling,

Stilling... your beating heart

Consider a life can find

Ebbing beats...

Beat-plead to live

Experiencing time

Being mortally sieved

Living,

Leaving... pleasures to mind

Wenlock Edge

There is beauty

To be found

At Wenlock Edge;

In green and limestone

Long lost reef

In fossil stone

Loud butterflies,

Springing meadows

Woodland walks

I found beauty there;

At the end of Wenlock Edge

Beyond Ippikin's lair,

Long buried treasure.

With her hand in my hand,

Though she already knew,

I tell her

That I love her

Cave

From blindness to sight

A tactile mouse man

He Clicks...

For live graven image

For visuals to scan

From virgo intacta

A woman placed higher

She Cries...

For the rolled away stone

For her missing Messiah

The sweet seventies man

Once a voice for the teens...

Unless I was...

Misshapen.

Sang Love is like...

exogene

(continued...)

All life craves a cave

He was born in a cave

His home...

Is a cave

A cave was the grave

.. was the cunt.

Of the risen...

Of the missing...

Messiah

But I'm Soaring

It's baggage isn't it?

All those pent up

Rent up

Hurts and perceptions

Mistakes

and deceptions

That litter us

Like discarded cigarette and plastic...

Non recyclable

And unfathomable

It's tragic isn't it?

As we hold on tight

To slights

Emotional abrasions

Those crimes

and frustrations

That pester us

Like those persisting 10p drunks...

Unacceptable

And embarrassing

(continued...)

It's logic isn't it?

As we made a choice

Rejoice

In deciding to soar away

From aches

And persistent sores;

Will resurface

Like occasionally unwelcome guests...

Ignored

Yet perennial

...but I'm soaring

In the sweetshop

From long trousers, to tall tales
Sweet humbugs, to humbug females
The sights, delights of the sweetshop
Never fails...

The boy's head, moves in delight
Left, right, left, right, left, right
The man finger-swipes on sight
Left, right, left, right, left, right

At lady-luscious sweet treats
Man and boy, a heart leaps,
But for a moment...
In the sweetshop

Ex and Why

As my ravenous, flesh feasting eyes

wandered across

That busy, bustling, busty room

Adorned by ex exes and invisible men

Very soon, and then...

I settled...

Unsettlingly..

On you

Unknowingly, or knowingly..

Provoking my why

You carelessly swooned my way

Regrets?

I have a few...

Maybe...

About you

(continued...)

When I first undressed you.

Though fully clothed

You smiled

As I smiled

My very best grin

Hiding the me

..bump bump bumping..

Within

That you might, very well..

Likely.. loath later

So, still hiding..

I unpeeled you

As object as an orange

Later

Shocked, unshocked

By a tone of farts,

And whining voice

Behind the bathroom door

The way you threw your knickers

On my bedroom floor...

When lovingly,

You spoke of love.

I was torn, in parts..

The kindness of your touch

Your eyes, your lips...

Versus your hidden fat arse

Where does it come from?

Your obviously,

Annoyingly...

Self critical nature...

On that glorious unwrapping day.

As you stroke my thigh

I love you..

You became my ex.

I don't know why.

Daughter

Of course...
I wish you strong
I wish you proud
I wish you confidence
I wish aloud
I wish intelligence
I wish charisma
I wish you kindness
I wish no stigma
I wish you healthy
I wish you love
I wish you blessing
I wish above
I wish your future
I wish it's good
I wish true beauty
I wish childhood
I wish you courage
I wish you hope
I wish you happy
I wish you growth
More than that...
That... true you are
Daughter...
To... who you are
Daughter...
I wish you... you
Unique and blessing
As you are...
I love you... you

Preacher

He stands...

As he preaches tall,

Smiling,

Slightly

Confrontational

Lightly...

Challenging

With his eyes...

He talks

Of judgement

Rebirth

Of love

Bursting optimistic

Pointing above

He's a good man

He's a righteous man

Aiming higher

That man

Of Messiah

(continued...)

Privately...

In the process

Of life.

Oh look...

He's just beaten his wife

Thrown Out

I was 17 when it happened.

As expected, as it was unexpected... that fragile, controlling, critical, unemployed bastard died.

Dad died.

It was unfathomable.

It was unfair.

I was angry.

Bitter, sarcastic, kicking, punk rock pogoing fucking angry.

And those bastards...

Self-made man uncle know it all says, 'You're the man of the house now'.

Shit.

I'm not sure that I even qualify. As a man, that is...

I don't even own a razor...

Or didn't...

I don't know what to do.

In the chapel, glancing across at my not so frail, frail grandfather dressed in dog collar black... I hold Mum's arm in mine. When she stretches her arm out towards the coffin, I resist. I think that's the right thing. I don't know.

Numb at the grave, angry forever after.

Two weeks on...

Mum's in the psychiatric ward, my four younger sisters staying with Uncles and Aunts across country.

Not me, I'm the man of the house now.

Sitting practising guitar, 'Please Release Me' on the steps of our council house.

Stiff Civil Service Manager, Mr Wood, comes to visit, to see how I'm doing, and disapproves... Bastard.

There were a lot of bastards in those days.

So I went searching.

I tried praising the Lord, with baptism, shagging, drinking, puking, fighting, arguing, drinking, puking...

I tried praising the Lord....

They excommunicated me 'cos of my shagging, or that's what I told everyone.

I was rather proud of them chucking me out, cancelling my church membership. 'Adultery!'

I didn't need them. Angry. Still angry.

And then Mum remarried.

Simple as.

She's 130 miles away, with half of my sisters and a Cockney Brummie.

She can't cope with all of us, much less a house of angry young child-man.

He didn't want me around.

So, eighteen months on, I sit and glance around my new place.

Bedsit.

Still Rhyl.

On my bed, glancing around at my worldly world.

Kitchen and sink hidden in the corner by 1960s curtain hanging from slightly greasy once-white wooden frame.

No money in the meter after a 'wild' weekend. Fags and beer, satisfyingly unsatisfying.

Thrown Out, not by choice. Not physically either.

Stifled by nurture – by criticism and control.

Desperately lonely, 18 months, from seven to one.

I'm the man of the house now.

he City

ʌre ye English?'

ɲfriendly, interested gaze met mine, amidst a snowy and cold Glaswegian
te December.

e was short, angry, yellow teethed, clad in leather... and indecipherable to my
ntrained, youthful, pierced left ear.

ʌas 20 years old, fresh faced and open eyed at unfamiliar surroundings.

/e'd just got off the train, and were desperate for a drink to warm us. The
imly lit, sparsely furnished cafe near the station was populated and guarded
y one of the largest cats I'd ever seen. And a group of young Scots, not much
lder than myself, one of them now questioning why I was there.

ne scene felt like something of a metaphor for my journey.

lo, I'm Welsh'.

)h aye? Ye sound English...'.

aving assured him that I came from Rhyl, North Wales and that accents in the
orth were somewhat different to the South, he seemed placated.

wonder to this day what might have occurred had I been English, but the
:ene reinforced my feeling of being alien in this strange land.

ars now pricked and defensive, I sat with her.

/ith unpractised small talk, we reassured each other as we warmed on two
ıps of tea. A single, small red suitcase, later to become a pillow on the
reets, held all her worldly possessions. Mine were all on my person. We were
elative strangers close to the end of our shared journey, from unwanted to
nknown.

We had known each other almost a fortnight. Later, she would become my wife, an ill prepared and unsuitable coupling, based on shared loneliness and fear. It was destined to end in a welcome, yet painful and guilt-ridden divorce from a surprisingly tender marriage where, in response to the world outside, she would drink and I would rage...

When our drinks were finished, I picked up her suitcase, and we wandered from the relative café warmth to the dark and cold welcome of the city.

We walked gingerly over the ice to find the George Square bus stop. I tried, surreptitiously, to take in the bleak, black surroundings of Hope Street. Reflecting our mood, our own need for painful and personal transition, this was a desperate, depressed city; once grand, still grand buildings time-painted a dark grey, as if to camouflage expectation.

It was 1981. It was the first time that I'd strayed so far from my North Wales childhood, this culture shock was frightening, yet exciting.

Standing and shivering at the lonely bus stop, I now had time to look around in the ever-dwindling light.

Statued and statuesque, George Square was impressive and dread inducing in equal measure. The stained, dirty buildings stood beautifully austere and uneven, like a hand of smoker's fingers, contrasting with the still falling, fresh faced snow.

The lights of an orange double decker bus pierced my thoughts... I don't recall the number. We got on gratefully, asking the gruff, yet kindly driver whether he would let us know once we arrived at Peel Glen Road. He nodded understanding, muttered back three times before we understood him.

We sat together silently, watching the twilight disappear, as the bus navigated through the wintry roads towards the West End of Glasgow.

Through the foreign familiar: Partick, Byers Road, Hillhead, Anniesland... I noted the names for future reference; streets showed quiet as the lights of our orange bus trudged through challenging conditions.

The Great Western Road seemed to last forever, but eventually I was woken from my avid, wary observation by another passenger tapping me on the shoulder.

We were in Drumchapel.

Alighting from the bus into unfamiliar senses. On the grey wall to my right, near the metal bus stop post, graffiti: 'The Peel Glen Team'.

In the gloom, we turned right, past a sign reading Drummore Road, the smell of piss on yellow snow. The sound of our footsteps carefully slushing through the wet, grey-white, icy deposits... was the only thing I could hear.

Walking up those eerily silent, narrow streets for the first time – 'Slush... slush... slush...'; flanked on either side by tall, blocky concrete tenements, I had the distinct impression of walking into a long dark tunnel towards God knows what...

In my enhanced state of intrigue, trepidation and fear, had the gates of Hades opened to us at that point, I may not have been surprised, only interested.

That thought made me grin, apprehensively, as I spied misspelt graffiti to my left... 'Welcom to Hell' and another... 'Fuck the pope'.

Princess Serian and the Lime Green Dress

Princess Serian was beautiful. She was always kind and helpful.

She loved doing things around the house, whether helping the woodcutter to chop wood or helping the cook in the kitchen.

Sometimes, in the lazy summer evenings after practising her swordplay with some of the local knights she would take a walk into the woods near the castle.

One such evening, as she walked on her usual path past a large briar hedge, something rather strange happened. The hedge shouted for help! 'Help!' it said.

Serian looked closely at the hedge, then realised that she could see a pair of dark brown eyes gazing sadly out at her. 'Help!' said the eyes. 'I'm Prince Eric and that awful wizard has cast a spell and left me here without any clothes'.

The Princess could see his cheeks blushing through the hedge. She looked away in case she saw anything else.

'Please help me find my clothes' pleaded Eric.

Serian sighed.

This was most inconvenient. 'Wait here' she told him.

Rushing home, Serian searched her wardrobe. Being a princess, all she had was lots of beautiful dresses. 'Oh well..' she thought and rushed one back to Prince Eric.

Eric looked out at the beautiful lime green dress that the Princess had brought with her.

'I'm not wearing that!' he said ungratefully, 'I'm not a girl'.

'Fine' replied Serian and started walking back towards the Palace.

'Okay...okay...' Eric shouted quickly

'No need to shout' grinned Serian as she passed the dress to Eric. She turned her back as Eric put her dress on.

'You look lovely!' smiled the Princess when she turned. Prince Eric had a very red face. He said nothing.

'Come on.' She told him, 'Let's go and sort that naughty wizard out.

The Princess set off with her new friend towards the wizard's cottage. She had seen her father King Freddie deal with this particular wizard before and knew that he was a bully who needed standing up to.

After some time, they arrived at a rather overgrown cottage. They might have got there much earlier, had Eric not kept tripping over the hem of his dress.

erian knocked on the door.

Vhoever that is, go away!' came a rude
nd muffled shout from somewhere inside
ne cottage.

he Princess knocked again, this time
nore firmly. Prince Eric moved back quietly behind her.

he wizard opened the door. He glared at the Princess, then he saw Eric and
ughed. Now, why didn't I think of that?' he chortled. Eric's face turned pink.

Mr Wizard..' began Princess Serian.

Away with you!' he shouted, 'or I'll turn you into a pot of paint!'

Mr Wizard' she repeated bravely, 'Will you please give Prince Eric his clothes
ack straight away, or I shall have to go and speak to my father about you.'

he wizard didn't look quite so sure of himself when he heard this.

he started again. 'Now, Mr Wizard, if you please...'

he wizard looked at his shoes. 'I'm sorry, Princess' he muttered. He leaned
ack into the cottage and presented the fine clothes that belonged to Prince
ric. 'I really don't know why I did it..' continued the wizard.

Later, as Prince and Princess emerged from the wood, Eric turned towards Serian.

'Thank you.' he said.

'It was nothing' she replied.

'You were very brave. Could I just ask you
something?' he said shyly.

The Princess turned 'Ask what?'

'Would you marry me when we're older, so that we can live happily ever after?'

Serian smiled. 'I can't' she said kindly 'I'm going to University when I'm older. And then I want to be a doctor..'

'And besides..' she added 'I'm having too much fun!'

Printed in Great Britain
by Amazon

49026080R00037